# Man's Wolf to Man

## Laurence W. Thomas

![PublishAmerica logo]

PublishAmerica
Baltimore

First printing

At the specific preference of the author, PublishAmerica allowed this work to remain exactly as the author intended, verbatim, without editorial input.

ISBN: 1-4137-9958-2
PUBLISHED BY PUBLISHAMERICA, LLLP
www.publishamerica.com
Baltimore

Printed in the United States of America

*Inhale deeply the aroma of peace;*
*take but a whiff of war.*
*--Al Abbas Ibn Merdas*
*(died 639 A.D.)*

# CONTENTS

# MAN'S WOLF TO MAN

I thought I knew the horrors of war from books and movies—when, at eighteen during WWII, I got drafted into what was termed "a popular war." After seventeen weeks of learning to hate "the yellow-skinned, slant-eyed bastards" of Japan, I was sent to Europe. If war had soured in my mouth before that, what I found in war-torn Berlin turned acid in my stomach. I had missed combat; what I was faced with was the slow process of recovery in human terms as well as rebuilding the physical. Buildings were empty honey-combs, scrabble piles of tumbled bricks and mortar. Below these, ordinary people struggled for survival against starvation, cold, and the indignities to which they had been reduced. Grown men scrambled after cigarette butts in the streets and engaged in black-market haggling over the prices of Leicas, Meissen, and whatever else they could dig up to barter for cigarettes, the accepted medium of exchange. Young men sold themselves and their sisters to GI's who could provide blankets, chocolate, and soap in exchange for sex.

Displaced Persons wandered the streets or huddled in camps like worms in rotten meat. The DP camp I visited was more demeaning to those forced to live in it than those camps for homeless Palestinians I was later to see in Lebanon, Iran, and Jordan, although they were miserable enough. If seeing your fellow man so reduced is not enough to harden your heart against war, imagine how Americans would react had we lost the war and the Nazis ran rough-shod through our cities.

With all our technical advances, we have made little progress in the art of diplomatic negotiation and compromise in dealings beyond our borders (and too often within them), resorting to preemptive strikes and devastating solutions irrespective of consensus. The battlefield proves an easier resolution to differences between peoples than does the conference table. Mankind should have advanced beyond the animal instinct to strike and kill when threatened; apparently, we have not.

Americans are naïve about what war can do to inflict disruption and suffering. We haven't had our cities sacked, masses of our people dispossessed, hordes of foreigners inflicting an alien order. Pearl Harbor and the World Trade Center, as horrifying as they were, pale in comparison to what happened to the people of Berlin, Dresden, London, Hamburg, Hiroshima, Nagasaki, and many other places in terms of human loss and suffering. I sometimes fantasize on what life in this country would be like had the Nazis fulfilled their goal of world domination or if one of the world's militant religious systems gained ascendancy and inflicted its philosophical opinions upon those whose beliefs lie elsewhere. Though I have encountered political and religious intolerance, living under such repression stretches the power of even the most active imagination. I am too attuned to the democratic process, flawed as ours may be.

War will continue to be seen as solution as long as financial and political interests profit from it. The prevailing philosophy that power emanates from above flies in the face of true democracy, and religious systems make no pretense of being democratic. But war should be the last answer—to be entered into only after all other efforts for accommodation have been exhausted. Treating with our enemies to prevent the outbreak of hostilities is much more difficult than attempting to repair the damages after their defeat. Benefits should be weighed against costs—to the participants on both sides of the conflict, those who wage war from board room or battlefield, and those noncombatants and innocents whose lives are overturned in the tsunami of war.

# AMONG THE RUINS

Where has the sense in all this chaos, order
once here, gone?  Neat rows of books
waiting for an idle hand on a dull day
lying spine broken and water warped.

A kitchen redolent with the aroma of a pot simmering
at the back of a stove grown cold, empty
as pantries littered with scattered bottles, hushed
as a table set and ready in a room with no people.

Walls, now crumbles of dust where once hung
artistic aspirations, a toppled chair
in front of a blank screen, a crossword puzzle
with gaping spaces waiting.  Piles of papers

shift in the wind across carpets curling
away from windows where house plants languish
abandoned by love and husbandry once lavished
with weekly watering, housekeeping now neglected.

Above, the emptiness of bedrooms, beds left
lonely, closets waiting with hangers rattling
like skeletons, echoes of resentment over neglect,
a cracked bathroom mirror reflecting on recreance.

All that remains echoes remembrance: sleeping
and waking, conversation and silence.  Soft sounds
replace everyday clatter: a step on the stair,
a floorboard complaining, the closing of a door..

# TRITINA FOR THOSE WHO DIE YOUNG

Successive generations come and go
but sometimes end before they've run their course.
The children would be saddened if they knew.

We say goodbye to many that we knew
too often prior to their time to go
because they failed somehow to stay the course

through accidents, disease, or war of course;
the older ones must bury those they knew--
the younger ones who should not need to go

and never knew they had to go that course.

# "MAN'S WOLF TO MAN"

Reducing ourselves to the animal levels
is not futile.
Unthinking nature reworks its materials
tearing down to rebuild from its limited stockpile
reusing the stuff of destruction.
Death that teaches how to live is not wasteful.

We have lost the art of trust,
suspicious of our friends;
what we don't know about strangers
makes them enemies to be dealt with
in the manner of animals.

Notably few advances mark progress
since the Greek golden era,
electricity notwithstanding or flush toilets.
We learn less about more
our success measured in self satisfaction.
We know more than Socrates;
history, however, still being measured
in wars and destruction,
our efforts today are not toward advancement
but how to stave off extinction.

We don't think so we aren't
any more than the beasts and we head
in counter directions.  We have lost
what we gained when Jesus preached healing
and Plato spoke to Thoreau.

# I THINK OF BELLEVILLE

*War results in a backslide.*
                    --Joseph Brodsky


Seen from above these honeycomb buildings
are like excavations of ancient cities
façades from a deserted set for a movie
where death and destruction are faked.

From below, walls with empty windows
of rooms perched precariously
hover above the tumbles of bricks
where doorways are dug into basements.

Girls and young women from respectable families
fall from necessity to exchanging gratuities
kids on the streets begging for chewing gum
their fathers dealing in black market cigarettes.

The trees on the avenues are trimmed of their branches
and then disappear as winter progresses.
By spring, the parks are shadeless and barren
with statues only; the pigeons are gone.

Arrogant armies looking for women
raid what is left of bombed out apartments
leaving the terrorized elderly hungry
cowering in their ruins of memories

while the ballerina still soars
in the cold that moves into the audience
shivering in overcoats when the curtain
rises and the lights go up on illusion.

# INNATE

Beasts supreme in their territoriality
defend what is theirs instinctively.

Big fish do not hate their prey
nor minnows those whose hunger they satisfy.

Birds and squirrels contend
over available food.

Animals cannot argue; they strike--
their monstrous egos blinding them

like men;
it is easier to strike than talk.

# THE UPS STRIKE

'How incredibly selfish'—my first thought along with the ignorance that sparks all strikes resulting from the inability to compromise--brings to mind small children screaming "I *want* that" whether they really need it, ignoring the question of how the expenditure will affect the family budget becomes, to the strikers, more important than what happens to businesses, nationwide, that depend on UPS. When children get out of line, they get punished, the quick alternative to reason--like waging wars--like going out on strike. People forget, in the momentary urgency of self interest that children grow up.

# LADY CROSSING A STREET

### --a neutral political allegory

She showed strength, courage
enough to brave the unknown,
that first step from the curb
into the buzz saw of commerce.

She thought the crossing
would be like at home
where drivers slowed for pedestrians.
She ignored the traffic signals

and, because her eyes were weak,
she couldn't see the other side.
Others looked for safer ways
to cross, but she was in a hurry.

She failed to note that in this artery
with cars coming from all directions,
the rules were different.  Drivers
were hell-bent toward accomplishing

their own agendas, and one lone lady
was only in their way.  Boy Scouts,
knowing the dangers, declined to help;
the local constabulary slept.

And so she ventured out, resolute,
because her family had not warned her
about life in the city, that there
are other ways to get across a street.

The brave lady didn't ask for help
and half way across she heard warnings
shouted at her, but it was too dangerous
to turn back, too deadly to proceed.

## WE ARE A SAFER NATION

When I hear that,
                    breathing easier
is like being told most sharks don't bite
as I put on my bathing suit.

I am glad I'm not from a family
                              with many sons.

# PASSING THOUGHT

The windows are broken, the students all crowded inside,
computers lie useless, equipment is missing, and teachers
have left for the suburbs to earn enough pay to provide

for their children. The trash on the street is crawling with
        creatures;
the buses run late and the service infrequent while inside
the old houses the drug trade increases in spite of the
        preachers

who close down their churches as population decreases.
Affected adversely, businesses default on their taxes
so the purses the councilmen relied on are empty. Releases

mean fewer policemen, and firemen lay down their axes
which puts people at risk of losing their homes and
        possessions
while the arsonist lights up the town and the burglar relaxes.

The mayor, in addressing the council in one of its sessions,
asks, "Where has the money gone? There used to be more."
"The answer is simple," one answers "Forget the digressions.

"The wealth of our nation has all gone to war."

# JUST DESERT
### —A Ballad for Auden

O, what is that rumble from so far away?
Whose are those voices screaming, screaming?
They are only some Arabs at play,
Some oil sheiks dreaming.

O, what are those pictures of rising smoke,
Those masses of people running, running?
They may be some photographer's joke
About cities burning.

O, why are our forces amassed in the sand,
Our ships and our planes converging, converging?
We must give our trainees a helping hand,
Our forces emerging.

O, what are those maps they show on TV?
The blue and red arrows flanking, flanking?
Only the officers letting us see
How they earn their ranking.

O, why are the diplomats not going there
With their golden tongues all flapping, all flapping?
Why, they're on the campaign trail, dear,
Or perhaps they're napping.

O, what are those stars in the Baghdad night
Like comets of doom that rise, that rise?
Just testing to see that our ordnance is right
Or to give a surprise.

O, why are our airplanes flying so high
Over the borders this morning, this morning?
Those are just test patterns in the sky
Or perhaps a warning.

O, why can't the journalists get in to see,
To send us reports of the action, the action?
They're permitted to encounter the enemy
But just a fraction.

O, why are those scuds arcing so high?
Why are they aimed at our allies, our allies?
Our Patriots will clear them from the sky
To even the tallies.

O, why are you wearing that camouflage suit?
Where are you going with those orders, those orders?
I feel I must follow the established route
To protect our borders.

O, it's gone the way that history teaches--
On brute force and murder relying, relying.
Ignoring the things that common sense preaches--
And people are dying.

# CONCILIATION

We have been schooled to kill
smugly totting up body counts
cosmetic blood smearing the village streets.

For those of us on the side of good
using a gun is justified
a battle better than compromise.

We make profession of thou shalt not
but never love our enemy until
we end up loving no one.

Cities lie with teeth missing
like prostitutes' skeletons
bred from a disinclination to bargain.

We wallow in our sad departures
at airports and cemeteries.
It's not the ones in body bags who suffer.

Cold slabs of glorification
mount still warm bodies
to interrupt the spasm.

We wave our banners in the streets
escape to where we hide the shame
without changing anything.

# CATASTROPHE

At the emergency center, set up to treat
ambulatory victims for broken bones
and gashes, in the high school gym,
survivors asked in anxious tones
after friends and loved ones.  In the street
they consoled each other, exchanging grim
tales of the carnage among the dead
and wounded.  Ambulances screamed away
adding their terrorizing wails to the night.
A disheveled couple embraced where they lay
moaning, but alive.  He surveyed the sight:
"It's a miracle we weren't killed," he said.

# CONFUSION

On the billboard, a smear of patriotic colors
fluttering like a flag, a symbol imposed at birth
and never challenged till someone pulls it down.

Along our highways, "God Bless America"
is superimposed, three buzzwords
aimed at urging everybody to do

something. Salute? Pray? Pledge allegiance?
I could do all three and feel good
relieving me of other obligations

like what—enlisting in the military, buying an icon
to hold reverently when innocent people are dying
or giving money to indeterminate causes?

Other wars were not like this;
we mobilized our forces. Many got drafted.
We had scrap and paper drives, shortages and rationing.

Men died in Europe, Asia, Africa
and oceans between. Stars hung in our windows--
white for those still serving, gold for the dead.

Now, we are told we are at war, but where is it?
What are we supposed to do, our lives unchanged—
sing anthems, honor the flag, kneel before icons?

# A HOME AWAY

Our tour to the Baalbek ruins is weather bound
the tour guide glad for the shuddering hovels
       corrugated tin and packing boxes
       old Coca-Cola signs written in French and Arabic
that line the road through the land of milk and honey
glad for the numbers of refugees of West Bank occupation
shuffling through the frozen mud
to help push the bus through drifted snow.

Back in my Beirut hotel I ask
       Who are the Palestinians?

# THE DISPOSSESSED

They saved whatever they could,
the dispossessed—their homes
in ruins, villages gone—
they saved few things
besides themselves
with value only
to their owners.

You cannot sell,
however rich your blood,
ancestral portraits
and survive in camps.
Who needs,
with villages like yours
proliferating throughout the world,
the burden of another child?

# PASSAGE TO CORFU

During the *Feria del Levante* in Bari I ask
an American ex-pat about the hammers & sickles
--it takes only one person to paint a town
he tells me which doesn't explain the hundreds
parading with red flags the next day. I am waiting
for a boat to take me to Greece.

From my hotel I watch fireworks romanticizing
the harbor from the end of the pier
where during the waiting I hire a small boat
to sail out among derelicts, a mini-odyssey
with my Charybdis, the even surge of the Adriatic
a half-sunken battleship my Scylla.

The town hasn't recovered from history
scanning the harbor, the source of its wars.
Its welcome is humble with no fuss
over arrivals by rail nor departures by water.
I have found a Greek diesel heading for Corfu
(deck passage only, no water or food)

with a captain and mate and three fares:
an elderly Russian in search of her family
lost in the war, and the wife of a minor official.
I buy a few apples, some bread and ham
and chianti to last overnight
but the crossing takes longer than that.

The trip across is hard for the queasy
though the sea is only hummocks and furrows.
The captain offers me rusks and warm milk.
I awake in Albanian waters still heaving
with no shelter afforded by these hard barren rocks
no relief from the oil-sick odor

till deep in the second night of our passage
we reach harbor. The little old man from the hotel
who guides me through sinuous streets
serenaded by hundreds of cats tells me
--we love our cats; toward the end of the war
we had none. The Germans had eaten them.

# THE END OF DREAMS

Wistfully, fingers unfurl along edges,
curl around corners, appraising
the value of treasures and visions
caressing here curtains, there
recollections, assessing the contents
of cupboards and prospects
prompted by envious urgings.

Alarmingly, tongues lash out
finding fuel for their arguments
licking at pictures
laughing at luxuries, leaping
from bed to conclusion.
Things loved too much perish
and a dream becomes reminiscence.

# EVIDENCE

Our arguments were never harsh enough
to make us less than friends, but we had them.
"How'd you feel," he'd start,
"if you got pulled over to the curb
or refused service, all because of your color?"
"I don't know," I'd answer.
"I've never been black."

Then I'd get back at him, or try.
"What about our freedoms?" I'd ask.
"We can go anywhere, say what we want,
choose our careers, practice whatever
our individual beliefs lead us to.
"I have no idea about all that," he'd claim.
"I've never been white."

"In Heaven," he'd argue, "Saint Peter
at the gate doesn't judge you by your race
and treat you worse than others.
God never says, 'You're black;
you gotta spend Eternity in your place.' "
"I wouldn't know," I'd say.
"I've never been dead."

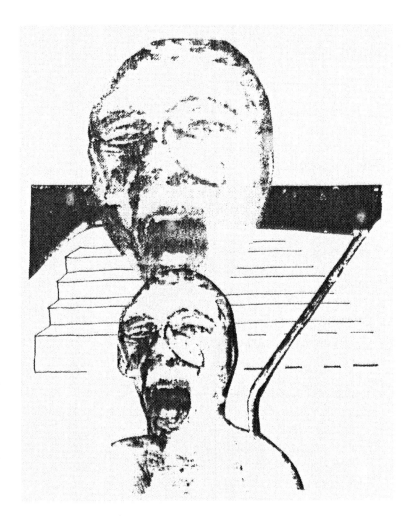

Epitaph for a Nursemaid
Black and white collage
by Judith Jacobs

# EPITAPH FOR A NURSEMAID

Belike the transformation came
to thousands like her,
sudden, irremediable,
a distant rumble or a speck on the horizon
considered or ignored,
welcomed with uncomprehending deference
and regarded as
nothing so very revolutionary.

It really was no change at all
except in names alone, for them
and her, of course, who died.
Distantly she watched, remotely
over fences, perhaps, or in parks
discussed with vaguest apprehension,
but she had her place
however much they struggled
over ideologies and who would hire the nursemaids.

And so she died, a symbol,
not for causes and overwhelming reforms
but because to get a perambulator
from the upper town
one must descend broad steps
with care
to the proletarian dockyards.


[In Eisenstein's film, *The Battleship Potemkin*, a nursemaid
with a perambulator was killed on the October Steps, caught
in a revolutionary situation.]

# EVEN ON CHRISTMAS

They didn't know the season,
those who left their homes
not for shopping in tinsel and lights
with carols broadcast
or for visiting grandmother.

They took her with them
if they could.  Their tinsel
was barbed, and their only light—
a rocket flare
hanging in the East.

.

# RAPE OF THE INNOCENT

1. The War Room

We have always known the nagging need,
an itch when scratched
returning for redress. Secretaries
of Prudence, Reprisal, and Internment
meet and issue warnings but the itch persists.

Fantasies conspire to convince us
that friendly gestures signal assent,
ready for a casual hand upon the knee
as we conjure up conditions favorable
for assault: some suitable spin

or warping to lure into our lair
the unsuspecting, possibly the innocent
with discreet diffusion of disinformation
to bolster our cause. Add low lights, soft music
flowing, and some behind-the-scene dissembling.

2. The Assault

Shock comes only if the subject feigns innocence
of what's coming, awe is inspired by admiration.
An all-out assault, with flanks exposed, caught
off guard or unsuspecting, might work like
going right for the groin with superior force

but the risk of unsuspected weaponry is great.
A subtler approach seems beyond question,
treating with the mark after the fray begins
like sending ambassadors into the line of fire.
Attacks thrive on weaknesses to gain the day

not diplomacy which requires concessions.
We seek surrender, to have our way with a foe
who would become our friend. Predictable
resistance, maybe from unexpected reserves,
comes from groping into unfamiliar territory.

3. Victory

Thrust against thrust, after aggression, retreat
to a conditioned submission that exhilarates
and calms—they to acceptance of our terms
and we to the satisfaction of compliance
that rewards both sides after hard combat.

The question, in doubt during early forays
when strength is pitted against greater force,
gets answered. We look for acquiescence
if not surrender, acceptance of our advances
made to bring satisfaction to both contenders.

And when the day is won and the sides sue
for peaceful cohabitation, like lovers discovering
mutual virtues, we rejoice. Like lovers remembering
past offenses, we indulge in recriminations, stock-piling
them away squirrel-like against another harsh season.

# NOBODY SAW

Slogging through the red mud of Arkansas,
our basic training designed mostly
to rouse our bile against the Japs,
we heard rumors making the rounds.
"Yeah sure, a secret weapon!"
We'd all read Buck Rogers when we were kids.

Nobody saw in that incandescent flash
the world turning a corner
sharper than any the comic books foretold.
Even Flash Gordon never saw the fear
his super weapons instilled, the rapacious greed
of the power hungry.
Nobody saw.

# GRANDMOTHER

My grandmother died in World War II. I would like to describe her parachuting into the Italian Alps or how she died on a beachhead on Guadalcanal. She never suffered the indignities of basic training, the steamy jungles of the South Pacific, nor cramped shipboard quarters. I can see her darting from building to building in village warfare or desperately reaching up to clear a space as she surfaced in burning oil after her ship was torpedoed. All that was left, however, to her offspring. We were all in the Marines, the Army, the Navy, or the Coast Guard, doing things Grandmother could never even imagine. She died peacefully at home during World War II, like most women of her day, never knowing what it was to fire a weapon in anger, to dig a slit latrine.

# TAUGHT BY EXAMPLE

Pour into the streets because we have not been shown--
have never learned the way democracies can shine

nor how to find legitimate ways to direct our wrath
when our system allows verdicts we disagree with.

Reduce to rubble places like Vietnam, Panama, Iraq
from the invincible strength of numbers and high tech

to force them to compromise their way of thinking, an irony
not found in any of the high-flown tenets of democracy.

Overkill is how to demonstrate that strength is the only way
in the face of the rag-tag ruffians of anarchy.

Send the marines in blackened faces and camouflaged suits
to deliver groceries to hungry people in dire straits.

Picket Kroger's because we have never found a way
to sort out differences.  Leave our classrooms empty

from lack of ability to teach accommodation
because give and take is a difficult solution.

Learn from Congress how not to get things done
to move the country forward, and never cross the line

of party affiliation nor shift from your stated position
unless such change will benefit your condition.

Kill our enemies because that's the easier solution
as long as we maintain our ethical compassion.

We know from television that the good guy always wins;
no matter how much blood is shed, the ends justify the means.

# EXCEPTIONS

"Thou shalt not kill," we hear at mothers' knees
except in war when anything's all right
so we continue doing as we please.

We want protection, give to our police
the power to kill transgressors in the night
in spite of what they heard at mothers' knees.

We feel much safer if a robber sees
we have a gun to guarantee our right
to carry on in doing as we please.

Deterring criminals with penalties
of death is practiced still--in spite
of what we should have learned at mothers' knees.

To educate our children guarantees
abortions will no longer violate
our need to carry on just as we please.

We pay lip service but everyone agrees
there are exceptions to the rule despite
"Thou shalt not kill," as taught at mothers' knees
and we continue doing as we please.

# VIDEO CLIP

Two people meet.

Their embrace suggests tenderness,
not the conflict
                    in the title.

Bathers splash in the shallows
like grunion.  Vacationers doze

away from their worries
            ignoring the laughter,

the possibility of sharks
                        or treachery.

A benign day.

In the dunes
the couple
            couple

like shrimp in cocktail sauce.
A knife flashes.

The camera pans
to a white cottage.

A leg of lamb
simmers in its juices.

Liberation
Black and white collage
by Judith Jacobs

# LIBERATION

Are these not the children flying now
in their shattered street around a pole
who yesterday were stealing tattered
through their street resentful and afraid,
their hunger gnawing with a rusting blade
these aging ladies?

Was their game today not played before,
an outgrowth of their need to celebrate
and soar above their battered street—not played
from joy but fear of what is circling below
these ancient ladies?

And do they know the games that other children play
along their scattered streets, choosing sides
and playing at a game of tag or war,
or is only swinging round a pole amusing for
these dying ladies?

# REPETONS FOR PEACE

We were taught to love our enemies
but that was before our leaders
taught us we should kill them, so
we learned to love to kill the ones we love

but that was before our leaders
revealed an evil axis separating friends.
We learned to love to kill the ones we love
and not to love the ones we kill.

Revealed: an evil axis separating friends
from those who pose a threat
and not to love the ones we kill.
Does religion teach us to love

even those who pose a threat
so we can inflict mass destruction?
Does religion teach us to love
only those who join us in the chase

so we can inflict mass destruction
on the innocent and guilty alike?
Not only those who join us in the chase
but those who become our victims

teach us we should kill them, so
we can prove the power of love.
We are taught to love our enemies
to death to bring about a lasting peace.

# FINAL VICTORY

Events so affecting this city erupting are distant in miles but not in spirit: this local team handing final defeat to its season-long adversaries. Celebration is in order; these celebrations lack just that. Streets fill as the last ball whooshes through its hoop; crowds gathered in bars and arenas to watch large-screen televisions issue out like children after school. Riverfront fireworks are guttering candles compared to explosions in streets of burning, overturned automobiles. Whistling rockets rising are a piccolo played pianissimo heard against ambulances rushing to rescue those injured, fire trucks wailing their dirges toward fires. Drums beating out victory rhythms are dim echoes. In parades, television eulogies, speeches by dignitaries, players, coaches, a voice is heard in one of those inexplicable silent moments that sometimes come. "I wish you the joy of the worm," it says.

## BYSTANDERS

Each of them has a personal formula,
a prayer or incantation,

some egoistic delusion that makes them seem
a part of the struggle.

You'd think they had taken the field
the way they explode

into the streets when the final whistle blows
rubbing the noses

of an enemy they've never met into the steaming pile
of its failure, a foe

who, instead of limping off with sad faces,
should be the ones

tearing up the town but joy is reckless, and defeat
ominously silent.

# GUIDEBOOK TO PURSUING AN AGENDA

First, don't just sit around waiting for others
to pursue their agenda
                           cut 'em short
beat 'em to the draw
and when they blink—pow
                               right in the kisser.
Give 'em all you got
                         (and some you don't got—
making sure you have unlimited amounts
of somebody else's money)

If they strike first
                     go for their balls
and squeeze, hard, till it begins to hurt
but don't wait for them to cry
                          *UNCLE!*

Instead—step 2: unleash your fury
on some nearby neighbor
rich enough to ensure
                     a big payoff
telling everyone he's guilty.
Make up stuff
                if you have to.
Patience is not a virtue.  You can't sit around
waiting for everyone
                     to rally round your flag.
You can bet your bottom dollar (not exactly *yours*
of course)
that someone'll kowtow
to your disinformation.

Tell it like it is
               making sure the numbers
favor the good guys: that their dead
outnumber ours and those who suffer most
dismemberment
               are the enemy.
Encourage the free press
as long as it ours
               and not anyone else's.


Step 3: Ignore advice; be a leader at all cost
so's not to be called a wuss
nor nothing like that
               so stay the course;
once in, it's hard to get out.


So—step 4: always keep your agenda
squarely in front of you
               but don't tell anyone.

The Lucky Dragon
Black and white collage
by Judith Jacobs

# THE LUCKY DRAGON

The men of science turn the golden page.
The fishers leave to cultivate the sea.
Sing loud the coming of the peaceful age.

The Lucky Dragon clears the harbor to engage
in age-old harvest action, as they flee,
the men of science turn the golden page.

The other dragon roams the islands in a rage,
lays eggs, so in their final hatching, we
sing loud the coming of the peaceful age.

The Lucky Dragon's sailors disengage
their engines off Bikini, do not see
the men of science turn the golden page.

The other dragon, restive in its cage,
struggles, suddenly emerges and is free.
Sing loud the coming of the peaceful age.

The meeting of the dragons sets the stage
where scientists and fishermen agree
the men of science turn the golden page;
sing loud the coming of the peaceful age.


[The Japanese fishing boat, *The Lucky Dragon,* was caught
in the fallout of the atomic test on Bikini and the fishermen
were killed.]

# WHAT MIGHT HAVE BEEN
--a treatise on tragedy

I'd have to know more about the lady crossing the street
to decide. What could she expect if she was careless
and pushed the baby carriage into the path of traffic?
The baby, of course, expected nothing. It died
ending the mother's plans for her child, so to her
at least, the small death was tragic. Parents should never
have to bury their children. If Friar Lawrence hadn't
       meddled,
the lovers would have lived to mourn their parents' deaths.
Tragedy is when what might have been doesn't happen;
or when what could have been avoided isn't.
Had I known them better, I might have understood
what distracted the lady, why the driver was in such a rush.
Where is the catharsis when a mother drowns her children—
for her, or us who mete out punishments? We trace
the tragic flaws and ignore them, altering our laws to fit
a procrustean bed willed us by our disinterested forefathers.
Antigone had choices: bury her brother and flout the king,
give in, leave the scene, or change the law. Her flaw—
ours when we place personal choice over popular demand.
Sudden surcease hurts. When plans are thwarted we cry foul
and seek redress for grief without acknowledging our part
in the bombs' dropping, the innocents' deaths, the tragedies.

# EXCUSES

When planes crashed
into our front yard
on a blue morning
of horror and surprise,
we lashed out
as we did sixty years ago--
how few remember.
We knew the yellow faces
and little else of the enemy
as we turned west, then east
to Europe and Africa
where the pot already boiled.
Parallels to war on terror
seem few. Now we look
for excuses.

After bombs dropped
into our backyard
on a blue morning
of infamy
we didn't need excuses,
excuses to retaliate
against those engaged
against us.
Now, with no clear targets
we invent them,
creating new
backyards and front yards
to drop our bombs
on blue mornings
of horror and infamy.

# PRAYER IN PEACETIME

What we need is a really good war,
the kind we used to have, you know, one
that kills a lot of people and
stimulates the economy with overtime,
manufacturing things we can't use:
planes, tanks, ships, and stuff
to fill army surplus stores for years.

All I pray for is another successful war
like Vietnam to show us who our allies are,
friends we can depend upon.
We need only to expand our dalliance in Iraq
to include good neighbors like Iran
and our Arab and Jewish friends
to reap the benefits of a good war.

Really good wars, like WW's I and II,
Contribute to reducing overpopulation,
our most pressing problem again today
(like 6,000,000 Jews, Dresden, Nagasaki & Hiroshima)
while ridding our cities of unsightly reminders
of a peaceful past. Without such wars,
we can never know what is meant by peace.

# PERHAPS TO DREAM

We weren't asleep but dreaming while awake
when hatred reigned and made us recognize
what seemed a nightmare yet was no mistake.

We let ourselves be turned aside and take
for granted attributes that we should prize
but lost because of dreaming while awake.

Suddenly we learned the awful ache:
destruction, death before our very eyes
that seemed a nightmare but was no mistake;

assailants hatched a dreadful scheme to break
our spirit, forcing us to realize
we must not sleep nor dream but be awake

to an evil, calculated threat to make
us live in fear, suspicion, hate, which tries
to drown us in our nightmares, no mistake

so now we understand just what's at stake
and rush to our defense, no compromise.
We weren't asleep but dreaming while awake
what seemed a nightmare yet was no mistake.

# PICTURES

The pictures on the screen, in tabloids
nearly convince us.  There's the proof
if we need any beyond all the spin

that our tax dollar
wields more clout than our vote.

We see our troops in a fire fight
always winning, bodies—ours and theirs--caught
in a rictus of victory—theirs or ours—

handled with greater respect
now they can no longer fight.

A pang pierces the heart of a woman
whose face is rarely shown—in Springfield or Tikrit—
and we become less convinced;

the thousand words
should have preceded the picture.

Shock and awe in living color bloodies our faces
as we watch with the guilt of satisfaction
neighborhoods being reduced to smoldering ruins

without the inconvenience of concern
for survivors, if there are any.

Images of war machines lying derelict,
bombed  buildings buzzing with death
bring home our involvement in distant places,

making us grateful that these are not
the malls and houses where we feel safe.

We have visions of our streets with smoke rising
from houses we no longer call home
pictured on the screen, the tabloids

of our friends and enemies
who watch with the guilt of satisfaction.

The stench of our rotting families
strewn about on once-familiar streets
rises to haunt our heightened imaginations

facing reality.  A wounded beast
is more dangerous than one running.

Picture us now lurking in ambush
with rockets launched and grenades killing
marauders come to plunder and ravage our land,

our muscles taut, our jaws set hard
in an attitude of grim determination.

# SIREN SONG

When young Ulysses heard the sirens'
treacherous singing, he had reason
to rejoice; courting danger, even wide awake
to jeopardy, rarely goes
unpunished, but he was wont to sleep

in peril, and in horses, ending wars. Reason
sits aloof from conflicts, puts to sleep
offending causes and effects the silencing of sirens.
Accord is lost, leaving in its wake
distrust, misunderstanding, when the envoy goes

away because he is disinclined to reason
at the conference table. The U.N. sleeps
its usefulness away and still the sirens
sound their warnings, and innocents awake
to wonder how the battle goes.

Flashing lights, horns, bells, sirens
alert those not involved to catastrophe, wake
benighted senses to dilemma, give reason
to count blessings as the saying goes
and turn to restless, troubled sleep.

Prepared for, trouble often goes
before it starts, giving way to reason
through the safeguard of being awake.
Though they disobeyed him, his men were not asleep
when young Ulysses heard the sirens.

When sirens awake, reason goes to sleep.

# THE UNSUNG

It's not the brave and valiant ones who strike a winning pose
on postage stamps, museum walls, and pictures in a book,
nor those who conquered everything, accomplished things
            that shook
the world, no, not to those this song of homage goes.

They've earned our praise, no doubt of that, and justified
            their fame
for all they've done to make the world a better place to live
through gallantry and vision, finding ways for them to give
to us a better living than we knew before they came.

But what of us, the little ones, who plod on day to day,
who buy the bread and pay the bills and give our children
            things
to make them grow to take their places next to us?  Who
            sings
our praises, we who never climb the heights nor go astray?

The villains, culprits, those notoriously flashing names
in headlines, claim attention more than millions such as we
who stay at home and keep our noses clean and never see
our names in print because we play such evil-minded games.

Receiving praise from those we most respect and love must
beenough to give assurance that our place is recognized
among the heroes; courage shown by anyone is prized
without the headlines, songs of praise, bestowed by history.

# WERE IT NOT FOR DEATH

Stand aghast at horrors, and fears
like ignorance will creep and conquer
culminating in the use of force

which settles nothing. Ours
is to question, not to suffer
from our inadequacies, wars

of our devising, or theirs
with whom we differ
and brutishly contend. Where is

the victory when bellicose ideas
are not abolished in the victor
nor the vanquished? What conquers

must be conquered from within: the powers
of death and ignorance, for
were it not for death, there would be no wars.

Printed in the United States
40035LVS00003B/70-117

9 781413 799583